Love Notes

Love Notes

© 2012 by Vagabondage Press

ISBN: 978-0615596716

Vagabondage Press
PO Box 3563
Apollo Beach, Florida 33572
http://www.vagabondagepress.com

First edition printed in the United States of America and the United Kingdom, January 2012

10 9 8 7 6 5 4 3 2

Front cover art by Kimi Kodate. Cover designed by Maggie Ward.

Love Notes

A Collection of Romantic Poetry

Vagabondage Press

Chaitali Deepak Gawade

BEGINNINGS

There will be many
beginnings,
no endings,
on this eternal journey
that we begin.

Dreams are made of
golden beaches,
sun-kissed skies,
dreamy eyes;
but mine are
made of you.

You gave out
rainbows
from your purse,
made paper boats
with hues of moon.

Tempted—
rivers turned course
to look at you.

I am just a mortal soul
powerless to resist you.
So here I am,
unable to stop
writing poetry for you.

Brigitte Goetze

OVERHEATED

A late afternoon sun covered the audience
like an electric blanket turned on too high.
The low rumble of the lecturer's voice,
slow and circulatory as a clothes dryer,
mesmerized. I, with my fountain pen,
blue ink spurting like steam
from an overheated pressure cooker,
wrote just one word
over and over and over again:
slanted, straight,
curved, upright,
plain, embellished,
underlined, encircled,
small, tall,
horizontal, vertical,
diagonal across the whole page
in big capital letters!
My neighbor's gray head bent
over my young shoulder. Reading,
he whispered conspiratorially,
"So, his name is Stan."

Julie Catherine Vigna

FIRST KISS

Their love is tremulous, fragile in its infancy. Honeyed lips brush
with breathless longing, the instant of ethereal sweetness causing
their hearts to tremble with timid promise. Peering through the
gossamer veil of years, I
still remember.

Frilled wafer enfolds
Virginal essence of snow
The blush of first kiss

Kayla Bashe

POET IN THE RAIN

Lost boy with blackboard eyes,
Itinerant poet subsisting on free food and latte fumes,
Neon ski cap pulled low over uncut bangs, hallway-bound.
Cold shade in a digital Hades of ambient guitars—
Don't look back.
I'd like to grab your pale wrist,
Offer you a riotous scarf,
Pull you to a warmer land
Of cherry trees, cartoonishly blue skies, big-band parades.
You'd find plenty to write about.
Cook you soup.
Who's the lush-haired, chattering girl who bid you
Wait outside in the rain,
Hands in pockets, brick-wall-slouched?
She is false sunshine.
She is no muse.
Your eyes are blackboard-dark.
I'd paint rainbows there.

Natalie McNabb

As I Am

How do you look inside me this way?
See the things hidden? Or so I'd thought.
The things I didn't expect you to understand.
How do you caress them? Put them back,
One-by-one? And love me just as I am?

Caitlin Meredith Walsh

THIEF

The moon's bright tonight.

Is it full yet?

Yeah. It's like silver glass.
Like a mirror. I could just
reach up and snatch it.
No one's watching me.
You could wear it on a chain.

You sound like you're
going to steal it.
Is that why you called?
Are you going to
steal the moon for me?

Maybe I am.

(I wish he wouldn't do this.)

(I bet she thinks I'm kidding.)

------silence on the line------

Hey, where did the moon go?
I was looking at it,
and my mind wandered,
and now it's gone.

See? I told you I'd do it.

Manda Frederick

YOUR CONFESSION

When your confession
I have to push you away
now toppled so far down

from you like a small
nested bird, I clutched

that shaking admission
strong against my core,

terrified to crush that
rapid-beating honesty.

Bradley McIlwain

CHERUB

So much to say about a bowl
of cherries

locked between lips—soft and
gushy

ripening years of our childish
love

unfolding over long summers.

John Byrne

AND THERE YOU WERE

A hundred thousand million seconds passed,
Close on behind a thousand million more,
When in the tightly, swiftly moving mass,
A second stepped aside and there you were.

And there you were, as ordinary as
A lightening flash. The second that revealed
You stayed aside; the others ceased to pass,
And all was still except a heart gone wild.

My heart gone crazy wild, you must have heard;
You surely saw I stared a million years;
I never saw enough and time concurred,
For it stayed stopped as everything came clear.

Yes, everything came clear, quite obvious:
No further need of time, once it made us.

Sharon Lask Munson

AUGUST NIGHT AT CRATER LAKE

Perhaps it is
the full moon,
or the wind

as it whispers
through spruce
and fir,

or the clouds
as they curl
over Wizard Island,

or the stillness
of this one starry night
that makes it ours for the taking.

Martin Willitts Jr.

FIRST LOVE IS BEST LOVE

First love is best love.
The winds are carefree women with baskets of white daises.

The elegance of the sudden ledge,
straight-down-dizzy,
where wet surface flat shale rock
and spongy-moss
makes us almost lose footing,
like love
reminds me how dangerous it could be
to miss what is in front of you.

And if you look, into the abyss,
you will find a longing
calling out to you.

Jennifer Smith

WATER SERIES

Water #0
the girl who loves you,
white curves of a wave in her
face, trouble to love

Water #1
underneath that blue
you could swim forever—if
you didn't drown first

Water #2
your bodies hidden
and revealed between water,
arms, here you are formed

Water #3
this love is the moon,
tide, superstition, blood red
waters cover you

Water #4
you cannot see your
reflection in that water;
she can't love that moon

Len Kuntz

TEENAGE SUMMER

The good thief watches while
we soak in a night-blackened sea of shimmering oil,
water that makes us weightless
even as you kick and paddle.
We'll be old soon enough.
Now the stars urge us to write songs or
yodel so that our laughter rifles through the sky.
The waves rock us like babies.
They slurp across our slick skins
and beckon us to kiss,
kiss deep and long
as lovers do.

Louise Blaydon

AT PADDINGTON STATION

There is no question between us, any more, of wanting:
I watch the way your lips move when you speak, your
accent falling sharp as shattered glass.
There is a foreignness to you, compelling,
in the consonants clipped off briskly behind your teeth,
that single crooked incisor imperfect and beautiful.
I want to learn the feel of it under my tongue.

There are no words for the press of you in my chest,
the swelling rise and fall of this elemental feeling
behind my diaphragm, over my heart.
Your hands, your hands, the strength of your fingers in mine,
The suggestion of freckles over the ridge of your cheekbone.
All these things I catalogue, remember.

I want to learn you.

Sweetheart—I use endearments without thinking—
there is no edge to this, no clean division
of what we were, and what we are becoming.
The buttons on your coat, your soft-tossed hair,
grass in our pockets on a London afternoon.
The echoing cavern of Paddington Station,
the sunshine:
these fragments line the lining of my heart,
this fierce light that threatens when I would speak.

I would have kissed you on the platform's edge
Had I known then, as now, you would have let me.

James H. Duncan

No First Kiss

I stopped before my hotel and
I turned to her, standing there with her dog.

I remember that this was the moment when
I should have told her that
I was in love with her, but
I didn't say a word.
I only stared into her wide beautiful
eyes and continued to be a moon
            hovering over her

Cooper Sy

SUMMER POETRY

Her voice is soothing regardless
communicating things that she knows
and I do not.

I want to enroll in her class
to sit on the first row and
stare at her face. I want
to show up at office hours
asking dumb questions
about Seymour Glass
and Paige Bergman.

My notebook is filled with lyric poetry
describing more accurately than prose
what it's like to find loveliness, smartness
hard-edged sarcasm, irony that burns
glaring resistance time and practice
have conferred on J.S. the status
of an expert.

Maybe I'll always be a student believing
there's time left for promises, forgiveness
two faces in the mirror that do not always
trigger the memory of *Persona*
And somewhere in the world
four feet, instead of two
are making tracks
in the sand.

Doug Mathewson

BREATHLESS

you exhale long
and I, in your arms,
inhale deeply of
oxygen-depleted exhalation
and get so dizzy
lying close.

Maggie Westland

FALLEN

I climb a tree.
In the grass of its leaves
I sit,
And watch you below.

The wind of your voice,
Unbalancing,
Pulls me downward.

Falling,
I fear hard earth,
And wonder!
I find your touch
Is soft grass.

Justin Blackburn

DEEPFREEZE

As we in different houses fall asleep,
Our toothbrushes sneak out
And meet down by the train tracks.

They kiss passionately
And create a glowing orange mist
That makes the ghosts forget they are deceased.

They spend the night together,
Our saliva they seek, bristle to bristle,
As we dream of the grapevine grudge
That refuses to let our missile explode in peace.

To think everyday we wake up
And the first thing we do is brush our teeth.

Aunia Kahn

SWEET SMELL

I laid on the edge, of the table
Watched the smoke rise across the room
The oven would sizzle, and make sounds
Although the light was broken, inside
He knew how to bribe me, many ways
A kind of sweet, smell that I adored
That of licorice, and dandelions
Embracing the table, dropping leaves
Encircled by the late ladies doilies
Stirring the pot, and air quickly
Catching the breeze, placing it inside
In table cloth patterns, eye focused
Hands manipulating the ingredients
Taste testing, heaven
Freshly washed hands, and cool lips
Handing me spoons to lick
Clean

Jennifer Hollie Bowles

TOKENS

As a child, I held your silences
close like best-friend tokens,
cherished the laughter of mercy-
playing, and delighted in the surge
of creek-jumping.

When you asked me to flat-top
my long-blond hair to match you,
I almost did because your voice
brought the tokens alive.

Hot tears galloped down my
face when you shot me in the foot
with your BB-gun ... the sting painful
like an omen of distance and years.

As a woman, I hold your silences
closer still, while the little heart-
shaped peach stone you gave me
rests in her wooden box, and the
memory of the sting becomes sweet.

Sara Harman-Clarke

LITTLE LOVE

To look down on your face from above,
to hear your tongue speak in a language
of love. You look up to a billowing sail
full and fat with content, and at that
moment when our eyes lock and I am lost
to all, I know that our love is forevermore.

John Oliver Hodges

SOMEWHERE IN GEORGIA

Somewhere in Georgia, she pulled over. We
stepped through the wildflowers to stretch
    our legs, share a candied apple, a kiss,
    a hug; then on my knees, my face
in the needles, around my ankles my blue
    jeans, I felt her pretty renegade lips,
        and the long blond hair, somewhere

in Georgia between the needled earth
and lights of the skies. Did the faces
    passing by see her sleight of hand?
    In traces she held me. I was helpless
in the wet grace of her tongue; and I
    drooled into this place, this carpet
        of pine, this lair, somewhere

in Georgia. In this posture I was bound,
    a tethered beast, dogified youth
    of willful surrender, to her body
married by the fire of her mouth. We
tarried here amongst blue-striped skinks.
    She bore me far into the woods
where, as I died, once more I was born.

Gabriel Valjan

FROM THE BOOK OF LOVE

Because of you I cannot read
The lines of my face
The curves of your body
Because of you there is a new language

Water is not wet
Air is not invisible
Earth is not solid
Fire is not hot

When you say nothing and everything
When you let me read your kiss with my lips
The one kiss that rewrites all my poetry

Joseph Wade

SWEPT

Hey Love,
I want a little sip
Of your sunshine,
A little nibble of your lips;
wanna crash in the waves
on the horizon of your eyes
and float in the clear blue warmth
of your soul 'til I'm wrecked
on the soft sands of your island.
I'm gonna build a fire there,
Keep it hot and high,
Name it—ours.

H. Edgar Hix

WHY I NEVER BECAME A LANDSCAPE ARTIST

When you smiled, and the teeth that lined your tongue
were brighter than any trees down any lane;
When your breasts were taller than any mountains
above any lake not so smooth as your belly;
When I found that the valley of your love
was brighter and darker than any canyon;
When we dressed, I heard words
tinkling out of my pockets and knew
I'd never be happy with dry, painted leaves.

Joanna M. Weston

DAILY PLANNER

when you say goodbye
in the morning
day breaks in my hands

I divide morning
into neat segments
     work them carefully
     to completion

afternoon slides
down a green slope
into your arrival

then time
is whole again

Isaac James Baker

EXPLAIN

I wanted to tell her I
love her this morning,
but she was sleeping
so soundly.

I'll go to work, I thought,
and think
all day long
of a way to
explain how she sustains me,
how I remember every single day
that's included a smile from her,
and how it seems all the
others simply never
were.

I'll try.

It would be easier
giving driving directions
to the moon.

Robert Scotellaro

A Brief Description of Heaven

I am waiting in the car,
a favorite tune
in my head. It's hot
and the top is down.

You're right on time.

First your smile,

then a pink pastry box
swinging from a string,

then your red dress
fill the side view mirror—

in that order.

Nikesh Murali

TODAY I SAW A YELLOW FLOWER

Today I saw a yellow flower,
Shivering in delight as the rain ravished her mane.
Naked leaves smiled mischievously
As the sky hid her blue eyes behind dark eyelids.
It reminded me of the first time I saw you...
You were standing on a sheet of dancing pearls
As the rain washed the colours off weeping willows
And dyed your feet lilac.
You smiled as cold streams of monsoon
Raced down your forehead to places of pleasure
And your lips red as blood, aroused by the insane downpour,
Opened to greet the love of the clouds.
Your eyes closed slowly as if to shelter this moment of passion,
Shielding it with your eyelids,
And your arms ran down your body searching for the arms of your lover.

Today I saw a yellow flower
Shivering in delight as the rain ravished her mane.
It reminded me of you
And the rain that brought us together.

Leila A. Fortier

LIKE RAIN

To
Read
You is like
Standing in
The downpour
Of a steady summer
Rain~ The kind that you
Want to dance in...Soaked in
Metaphor ~ Your stanzas cling to
My body and streak my face like the
Tears I dare not cry in splendor...And as
I spin...You stream and cascade whispers
Of revelation with sounds that resound like
Fingers tracing crystal and spoons tapping
Glass ~ Street lights shine iridescent flecks
Splaying off of me...As I whirl and as I
Dance in this trance ~ To the music
You make that I dare not
Sing ~ Reverberating
...Within me...

A
Rising
Crescendo
Of momentum
Breaking stillness ~
Splashing in pools of
Verse rising...And puddles
Are becoming like ocean's high
Tide ~ And I just want to be swept
Away by that wave ~ Pulled under
By the current and drawn into that
Place where your inspiration is born
And moment by moment ~ Breath by
Caught up breath is released once
Again beneath the light of a
...Milk white moon...

Gary Beck

MON AMOUR

You, who have given me
your sweet lips
and made no measure
of the loving gift
that brought me pleasure,
are cherished beyond forgetting
in everyday renewal.

Tetman Callis

MY LOVE

my love if you must scream
go out to the desert and scream at the stones
they will echo your cries and transform them into song

my love if you must bleed
take yourself down to the river
fill it with the force of your life flowing to the seas and oceans
become the waters of birth and rebirth

my love if you must burn
place your burning hands against my skin
wrap your fiery arms and legs tight around me
press your hot mouth to mine and burn me
burn me through and never let me go

Susan Milchman

LAST WISH

I want to kiss you.

I want to rake my fingers
through the silken surface
of your luminous moon.

I want to shed my soft rain
over the soulful peaks
of your silent, majestic pines.

I want to bury my heartbeat
in the brilliant, armored folds
of your crimson rose.

But mostly,
    my love
        I want to kiss you,
            again.

Len Kuntz

IF I WERE A POET

If I were a poet, I would
say things better,
string sentences across a window with a thick font
so you'd see me in a new light,
see how serious I was,
how tender I could be with this sheer
and fragile love of ours.

If I were a poet, I would reshape syllables and sonnets into
a song sewn specifically about the sound of your breathing when the stars
hang up on a night wire to watch
like so many bejeweled birds.

If I were a poet, it might make me a better lover,
less insecure and needy.
I might be able to shake this sense that you are in the closet right now,
looking for something to wear
while filling a suitcase for your escape.

Richard T. Rauch

APOTHECARY JARS

Your arms bring good medicine,
like apothecary jars

spectralizing sunlight
in a pharmacy window.

Your smile, prismatic, a sweet elixir
arcing through my mind, freeing rainbows—

Gentian Violet, Prussian blue,
rose petals, and calamine—

fixing me with tinctures—
cinchona, cinnamon, and sassafras—

bringing me back
from those cyanide blues

as animated
as a cartoon character,

as onomatopoetic
as *you.*

Daniel J. Fitzgerald

DRIVING SLOWER

She fell asleep
> in the car
while we drove down a highway,
taking her to some task
not of my choosing.
I day-dreamed of
romantic encounters
in exotic lands.
She slept unaware,
But then,
> I looked at her face
asleep in trust of me,
remembering two nights before
when neither or us
could find our way thru the other
to find the back of the bed.

I slowed the car a little.
to let the countryside
> drift by,
lulling her
> and me
into more blissful
> dreams.

Anthony DiMatteo

IN NEED OF ASKING

I want two or three tears on silk
The color of pools of fire fish
Buddhist monks feed as they near highest heaven;
And the smallest hairs from the small of your back
Shaped like the softest sluice of a waterfall
In the deep of a forest under a harvest moon.
And the scent of your mouth that spills over
The slender ridges of your lips, I will collect
In person, seeking your gift that you need give freely
Or not at all. These are the things desired
And the gentle way in which I want them of you.
Or is there a new discovery to add to my list?
Something else nearer your hidden soul
No one else must see unless love bids?
Humble before you I stand, proffering
Gifts of my strawman self, seeking your streams.

Benjamin Wolfe

A RUSSIAN SNOWFLAKE IN ENGLAND

A Russian snowflake fell in England,
White and beautiful
And delicate, like a pretty face.
And gasping,
I caught it on my hand,
Amazed that it picked me.
Now I must run around,
Protect it,
And make sure she doesn't melt.

Jean Brasseur

YOU ARE EVERYWHERE TODAY

You are everywhere today:

in the ray of sun that struggles
to meet my face;
in the slight pain
above my left eyebrow;
and in the corner of my heart
swathed in white sheets
and plastic dust covers.

I see you in the spaces
between my words
and the blue patches
between clouds.
You are even in the pause
between the ticks of the clock.

Touch me, please,
and I promise to pretend
it is just the wind
that makes me shiver.

Bradley McIlwain

SLEEP

She tells me to turn off the light—
I obey.

Her voice distant, dreamy—
words like warm milk

carry my body toward the sheets,
pulling me down into the darkness—

I tremble.
Her skin is soft like honeysuckle.

I hear no sound but the silence.

The night is ours for a while,
two figures bending in the dark

like branches on a willow tree,
making poems in the moonlight—

and for a little while the world closes
her eyes,

and for a little while night subsides
to night—

and we are, for just a little while,
and we are, for just a little while.

John Tustin

COME TO ME

Come to me on the night
That is mercurial and clockless;
On the night when I have eaten,
When I have drunk
Just enough.
Fall small and luminescent into the valley
Of my arms
And be safe and lost.
Let my arms enfold you,
Let my arms encapsulate you,
Let my hands stroke and guide you
Through the night without names
Or numbers.
I tremble before your eyes that see
The things that I cannot,
I yearn for the tongue of resplendent words
And of resplendent touch.
Your hands, these two perfect insects searching
The underbrush of midnight for the food
Of my soul
And finding it.

Kristi Petersen Schoonover

TODAY

In the shower, we wash each other;
mounds of Ivory soap eagle's wings.
We share secrets
as you slap on your aftershave,
and I curl puffs of cream on my legs.

Over eggs
we poke fun at ex-lovers and wonder
whether or not they kept our gifts.
You sip your coffee
and ask me
if I enjoyed the rabbit fur,
and I say, "Oh, that's what it was?"
Because my eyes were closed
in the glorious erasure of a yesterday
when I hadn't known you yet.

Susan Free

About Desire

Now I know what they mean when they say desire:
it is worse than a drink and a drink makes it worse;
the slight tremble, the fire in the cheek, all the clichés of the body's betrayal;
the curse, the dreams, the famine of touch.

How does a person act like themselves:
go about the acts of speaking, moving, breathing in and out;
not forget what their hands are doing;
not speak in a language they can't understand;
hear above the sound of their own beating heart?

Peter J. Grieco

COUP DE COEUR

Don't want to leave my bed-warm
thoughts, or the memory of her scent,
of my hand almost brushing her hair,

the richness of being cupped
in this fantasy of resting my head below
her chin or against her soft abdomen,

of following my nose along her hip.
There is a point in falling in love when
the lover will anticipate each ripple

of pleasure set off by the merest
of contacts, when to feel the glow of a cheek
glancing close will seem as much

as touching tongue to the sweetest,
most electric honey, all set abuzz
and lost in the amaze of being near.

Dave Migman

UNION

To press my lips
Against each freckle
And breathe with you
Our dance of tongues
Our nights of eyes
Our longing

All that is sundered, surrendered
in the musk-scented dawn
embraced by the shroud
we will have to return it

all this time is borrowed
from our glowworm guide
One emerald night.

Natalie McNabb

FINDING THINGS IN THE SHEETS

Afterward
we lie
    beautifully spent,
    content,
    entwined
in sheets.
We loosed
pleasure,
    fell,
    dove,
    were freed
for hours,
easy
at play:
    daring,
    teasing,
    amused grins,
like kids.
I found
myself
    and, in
    that finding,
    found
I wanted you.
And, I found
you
    hidden,
    waiting,
    inside
my heart.
I would
like
    to discover,
    uncover
    myself
in yours.

Roxanna Bennett

HUMMINGBIRD HEART

She wants to brand his pen name on her hidden
skin, undress him with her teeth, tongue her way
through the arc of his throat but he's forbidden;
she can't mark him for her own, pin him down, lay
claim, play coy. Powerless to expose, possess, she
can't withstand her own need. Obsessed, shown
her greed, grinding slowly, soaked, against his knee,
allows him to command, provoke, evoke low moan,
grip her hips, slip in a merciless kiss, feed her what
she knows will destroy her. All she can't live with.
Under his hands she's mute, thrall to torment, hot
shocks shoot through her hummingbird heart, frantic,
hungry. Shy of sudden pursuit, unnerving surrender,
she submits to the terminal love of a stranger.

Murray Alfredson

LOVE SONG

You live inside me like a poem growing
        from unseen deep,
like themes of music richly, warmly flowing
        through my sleep.

You stir beside me, nuzzling past my dreaming:
        our spirits wake
like kindled flames from hallowed hearths outstreaming;
        our bodies quake.

Sparks leap from skin to skin; fresh arts devising,
        our souls conspire
to build our love, our thoughts, our touch, all rising
        to one wave of fire.

Flames sink inside us, play round hot coals: glowing,
        we draw apart
and lie together, murmured warmth bestowing,
        clasp heart in heart.

Poem and music, sweet as incense writhing,
        sway in time
with waves of sleep that lull our four lungs' breathing
        to rested rhyme.

A. J. Huffman

Insinuations of Silk

I dream of writing
across his chest:
Anything
(in marker).
Soft and wet,
I'll blow it dry
with kisses and wishes
and sighs.
To make it fit.
Me,
A run-on to run off with
into the silence.
And the softest moon.

Laura Dennis

ORANGES

surprised at
the soft warm kiss
on the back of her neck
the half-peeled orange
tumbled to the ground
he licked
the sweet juice
from her fingers

Daniel East

THE STARS ABOVE YOU BEGGING FOR SURRENDER

You're going to the roof and out like the tide
and neighbours watch you glowing from their windows
where cat paws push the dust together.
Your hairs swing round you like the necklace
of an ancient race of birds,
so white from your tower,
over many miles to deserts shielding wells of tears.
Through gutters you lower the last names of earth,
while stars surface from a purple sea
and brush with silver tongues
locks of your unburdened whispers.

Christina Lovin

GENERAL SEMANTICS AND THE MOLES ON YOUR BACK

You turn away and lie with your back to me—
stippled skin stretched over the frames
of spine and ribs. I read the map of you,
a blind traveler tracing the topography—
plains, knolls, vales of your body—
a universe scrolled out on supple flesh.

I know your body like the road back home
where the way seems sometimes dappled
with shade from tall elms gone
since my childhood, lost to my vision.
Yet my stumbling feet remember danger
from roots half-buried, like that phantom limb
of my uncle who cried out and grasped
the pulsing emptiness beneath his knee,
feeling the pain of only what was missing.

The word is not the thing, the map is not
the territory. You are not you. You are not
here. Perhaps you are not at all. But
your fluid spine still flows north
from that lush valley. Three dusk-colored points
of sandy flesh— intricate as the pyramids—rise
warm between your shoulder blades: to their
mystery and between I fly and I am counted lost.

Alan Gann

OUR NEXT KISS

Our next kiss will be a jaguar crouched in a tree,
a bull seeing red, and we will divide the dark
like a diver splits the surface,
lose our way like echoes in a too deep well.

Tonight's moon tumbles from her perch;
lizards vanish at the root. Slither through
the thicket with me, and our next kiss
will be smoke on a burning river. Silent

as the library after midnight,
reliable as December's chill, I will come to you
and wrap your thighs in the fires of guilt.
Like the underside of a rotting trunk,

like a cat sleeping in the sun, our next kiss
will be opium from the pipe: slow as a heartbeat,
needy as an tomb—crawl toward the door, rise
and we will run deeper and deeper into the night.

Robert Wexelblatt

AN OLD PHOTOGRAPH

Of laughter there was ample, and flowers
flaming on the verges. The neighbors' mowers
annoyed you for an hour, and when
they stopped even your curls relaxed. Then
you casually lifted off your blouse
to feel the sun, and I rushed into the house
to fetch the Nikon and two pale ales.
This snapshot's worth a thousand drawn-out tales.

Liz Dolan

THE AUGUST PLACE

Mister Conklin's bay-hugged, dusty cottage
with the mildewed corner cot

in the small white room, but not
too small for us who lay

hip to hip in it. Warm, smooth skin
and misty breath. Salt-encrusted eaves.

The breezed, gauzy curtains billowing
above our heads. The sweet silence

of your shirtless self. Your crooked-up
arm beneath your head and I, yoked,

as we whisper in the hollow space of
Mister Conklin's bay-hugged, musty cottage.

Summer's demise would soon catch us
off guard and always we'd be heartsick for it.

A brown hair spare on a pillow
a red-winged blackbird window-ledged.

Anne Bastow

ONE WEEK

You've returned to my daydreams.
I am distracted by body parts—
shoulders, hands, neck—
your shell.

One silent week
in Bora Bora is all
I desire, walking unfamiliar beaches—
you in your mirrored sunglasses, me
wearing my insides out.

Robert B. Moreland

INTIMACY

Wild passion catches us unaware,
our very breath taken away
in a moment so surprised
at the joy of being
alive; nerves firing
in synchrony;
primal scream,
our souls
freed!

Then
after
cuddling in
afterglow's sweet
perfume, the stolen
afternoon a guilty
pleasure taken from work's toil
and laid at our feet quivering,
mixed with warm sunlit spring memories.

Stephen Busby

ONE NIGHT LAST WEEK

Something woke in me one night last week.
Was it you who lay down with me, wet, by the water?
You, whose clothes we left strewn across the grass,
Whose tongue kissed the centre of my celibate life?

Something woke in me one night last week.
With you, who ran with me in the woodland to the other side of the water.
You, whose browned breasts rose as I lay underneath you in the cool evening air, so blessed,
Open and trusting, kissed and caressed.

Something woke in me one night last week.
It was awake when the rain came to distract us in our stroking,
And you walked with me, slow, upstairs to the bed before the window,
Black hair falling towards me, eyes dark with something not said.

John Tustin

YOUR LIPS

Your viola voice.
Your body held together with delicate strings.
Your mouth that tastes of peaches and sweet tea.
Your mouth so delicious, I've only tasted it a moment,
A moment in time: I see a paper hanging suspended
In thick Manhattan sky
Just outside my eyeline.
I see the limbs of a tree
That seem to come alive with movement:
You stand on your toes,
Your eyes on me, your arms around me,
Your body frightened but certain.
There is a calm that belies the rush
Of robots in smart skirts, in suits
And ties rushing around us
As if they are scattering leaves.
They aren't there anymore.
The sun disappears.
I hold the moment as long as I can
But
You disappear.
I stand before the manmade waterfall
Holding myself, watching you go,
Not aware of anything,
Feeling myself, all the good
And bad things that I am,
Tasting your midday kiss
Of an autumn day, of a bitter cold evening
Under your quilts, above your soft and pliant body.
Your lips the lighting of a candle,
Your lips a solemn tune,
Your lips a thundercrack of clarity,
Your lips a delicious sanity
When nothing else
Makes any sense.

Tina V. Cabrera

Unadorned

As the silken length of red ribbon flatters the modest blank page—

> so the smooth angles of your body
> coax a blush to the unadorned
> surface of my skin.

Liz Dolan

THE SWEETNESS OF SUMMER

has reached its apogee
and has begun insensibly to wane,

and we whose love was spawned
and nurtured by the sea

sit knee to knee on the beach,
sand fleas pricking our toes.

Silently we marvel at a beige
and sage preying mantis

who alights on your thigh
lingers as though he believes

we will cool him forever
beneath our umbrella. Folded

pea green wings do not flutter
until we rise as thunder grumbles

and flustered gulls flee,
the heat almost too much to bear.

Katie Manning

DANDELION WINE

for Ray Bradbury

I thought you were twelve when I fell
in love with you for the summer.
I called you Douglas then, and I
chased your new tennis shoes across

fields of dandelions—flowers
that grown-ups used for wine, but we
knew the best trick was to pucker
our lips, let our breath make them fly.

I met you again by the beach
eight years later. It was raining
and cool as lime-vanilla ice.
The sight of your silver hair took

my breath, and when you held my book
in your hands, the age spots confirmed
my mistake. Douglas was just your
shadow—I was sixty years too late.

David W. Jones

TOUCH OF THE ARTIST

She sits beneath
Contemplation,
Enjoying the
Spring afternoon,
Reflecting on the
Subtle perceptions
He once painted
Deep beneath her skin.
Thinking about
His fingers, trailing
Sketches along her
Water colored realities,
Remembering strokes of
His touch erasing
The dark lines of
Her emotions.
Her desires becoming
Vibrant passions
Conceiving pleasant visions
Within her spirit.
She waits
Upon the canvas
For the artist
To return.

Joan McNerney

LAST SUMMER

Golden sunshine spilling
over cathedrals of trees.
forest of summer.

Your eyes are oceans of light
beams, of light soft beaming,
dancing through rivers of memory.

Forest of rivers
drowning in oceans of eyes.
Your eyes when sunset spreads
over sand dunes warm golden.

Stars gliding past heaven
as night explodes in
cathedrals of light.

We bed down together in
forest of memories,
your body so strong golden.
last summer with you.

Dave Migman

Sixty-Nine Nights

these long nights are as if
the blood of the world turned to ice

in the cupboard your clothes hang
they are scented
alone in the darkness
I hold them to my face

I kiss the cloth. Your absence fills me,
fills the room, fills your empty clothes
torments the space beside me in your bed

loving a winter star
so distant, just above the horizon

tears fall cold on my cheeks
the blood of the world
rolls down melancholy shores

Chuck Augello

VERONICA, 2006

I carried her breath in my pocket
Kept a photo of her shadow and showed it to friends
Found her profile in the outline of a storm cloud
Wrote her name in Chinese letters on the back of my hand
Sewed into a quilt her old grocery lists
Built a nest from her little red party dress
     Fell asleep, a skeleton dreaming of skin

Nikesh Murali

THE GIRL FROM GOA

I saw you today
from a distance,
through muslin
in the filtered light of a candle that became restless with your arrival.

I longed to touch you from across the scattered wares on the table—
the sea shells, the beads and the little thoughts of lust.
I longed to cradle your breasts in my palm
While your eyes listened to the sounds of the sea, so clear in this warm
Goan night.
I longed to sketch your body on the sand
Just like it is now—etched against the soft white sheet;
And to think that it is all that separates you from me...

And so I left in a daze and dreamt that
I saw you today
from a distance,
through muslin
in the filtered light of a candle.

Caroline Misner

BLISS

Words I wouldn't dare
say aloud,
uttered between whispers
of breath.

Where you should
be touched;

it's deception's
enchanted mistress
that keeps me whole.

I must believe
in bliss;
it is where you are
now, awaiting
the stroke of
an unfinished kiss

that will never come
again; desire that's
a thousand miles away.

I long to be
with you now;
that would be bliss
to me.

Elizabeth Ashe

IN YOUR ABSENCE

I walk around naked in your absence.
I am myself, with thighs
and breasts exposed to the steam
and crumbs of afternoon tea.
I paint and use my left arm as a palate.
I can't do this when you're here—
I make you think of sex
and philosophy, a balcony garden
meant to disrupt a cityscape.
I like this; the me-time
isn't lonely in your absence.
The grocery list on the fridge
is in my handwriting.
The last two lines are in yours.

Anjoli Roy

LEFT

It would be invisible.
Below the surface.
The tremors a muted vibration on land.
You wouldn't feel it through your feet.
Wouldn't be able to cup it in the curve of your hand.
But it would be there,
Dark and dim,
Where the genesis is.
Where love starts,
Where pain lives,
Deep inside the earth.

That's where you'd feel it,
If I left you
For good.

C. V. Hunt

THRESHOLD

I wait for you here;
In dreams I long for your touch.
A kiss I wish for,
Waiting evermore,
Wanting an embrace from love.

Mark Underwood

ON LEAVING MY SILKEN BEAUTY IN THE STRIKE ZONE

A puzzle so simple, I almost missed it
Only two pieces, only two slight pieces
So intricately curved,
When laid together
The joins became invisible.

Despite this slight of flesh, there was no sharp touch

None could have foreseen how well they'd fit,
Nor how incomplete I feel now they're parted by space and time.

(York Notes: I miss you)

Susan Milchman

NIGHT SWIMMING

He wraps her in warm ropes and folds her into his fluid shapes

of twisting need. He carries her down whispering hallways

and lowers her into his glimmering mirage. He strokes

her bare back with hands of sun, leaving an

ethereal trail of heat along her snake of bones.

With beauty like a sea horse, she curls her grace

around his feet and she swims. In his pool of fevered debris,

truth and treachery embrace in a gorgeous blaze, their bodies bloody

with familiarity. He kisses her with tender fury in the bending light, pulling

her into his window, the fractured frame holding it all together. He leaves

her carved and addicted, and says he will be right back.

He never comes.

Anne Whitehouse

AT THE WINTER SOLSTICE

The western sky flushed pink;
clouds blew over like smoke.
The trees stood still, as if carven.
On their branches glittered
tiny lights like jewels
threaded through bones.

Dead leaves rustled at our ankles
as we walked in the park,
our fingers entwined.
In the air was the breath of the river;
the river was the color of the air.

Our hands fell away like leaves.
How easily we cleaved apart.
There was no blood.
Ashes fluttered like insects
from a trashcan fire
started by a homeless man
to keep warm.

We said goodbye and never
saw each other again.

Richard T. Rauch

Open Window Open Book

You were more in the morning, less
than it would seem, but all I seemed to need;
or so the open window told me

in terse fugues tapped out by acorns
falling hard against the gutter cans,
curtains lilting on a soft breeze

filled with coffee and bacon smells—
wafting down the hall in song—hums
and whistles in lieu of certain lyrics—

amid pots and pans, while squirrels count up
their winter larder and house wrens squawk
ennui, ennui halfheartedly,

or so it seems to me. Pillows
never quite right, never enough
down for proper propping up.

If only I could freeze you
as you were, as you are, as I hoped
you would be. Eggshell ceiling dares

a blank stare, like this open book
that holds no words for me, unlike
your signature hints of burning toast.

Laury A. Egan

WAITING

A Great Blue Heron flies over
the white-capped bay and river.
I watch the bird returning
to her nest and envy her,
for I must wait for you another day;
the hours intervening
only half-filled with living.

Susan Free

WHEN YOU ARE AWAY

I make the coffee too weak.
I eat over the sink,
toss dirty clothes in the middle of the floor,
leave them for hours, then pick them up in disgust.

I stare into the refrigerator, save the good food,
even though I know it will not wait
for your return.

Jake David

WE'LL BEGIN, AGAIN

I don't know why I hold on to your memory
of what we never were, as we're going to one day die.
But for now, we're young: let's let ourselves
kneel before Honesty on trial,
and travel through the spirals of this February night.
Let's let our overlapping heart's hymns deliver
the crescendos and sonatas of Eternity's song, together.
It's foolish thinking we'll be together again,
but not as foolish as thinking we won't.

Lisa Jayne

CROWDED ROOM

Everyone looks the same,
But nobody looks like you.
From your walk
To a reflection,
My near sighted eyes
See you clearly.
Even before you've
Come into view,
With my back turned,
I feel you waiting
As you turn to go
And I never look.
It couldn't not be you.
And I feel like
We've felt without touching,
For hours alone
In this crowded room.
I have you.
And it hurts
When I realise
You don't even know.

Maude Larke

ABSENCE

When love forms a chant in me
and keeps me awake at night

only one touch forms itself
   within that song

my face knows
   a phantom caress

as light as the air
   from a wingbeat

as soothing
   as an autumn breeze

as vital
   as you are to me:

this mist of gesture
   calms the waking
      rhythms the song
         eases to essential peace.

Michael Lee Johnson

SANDY

I have seen your eyes roam
over me so many times,
I don't even bother to feel
them anymore.
One can speak with the eyes,
you know—
and you've been silent
for so long
it doesn't even hurt anymore
to see you staring at me
and not uttering a word.

Andrew J. Lucas

SILVER STAR DREAMS

I spent a frigid winter alone
Sheltered by stacked mountain logs
(Dove-tailed four or five high)
Comfortably boxed around me.

Gazing over a snow-cloaked valley
Through a crystal-glazed window.
(Wiping frost, like tears, from the pane.)
Often, I thought of you.

My mind watched you,
Memory another wintered pane.
(Exhaust rippling across the tarmac.)
Ice dimpled beneath your heels.

A cool breeze tickles my eyes
As I pull closed the curtains,
(You trimmed in blue with white lace)
Turning to restock a dying fire.

Cocoa warmly cradled in cool hands
I settle into an easy chair,
(Warm and cozy enough for two)
Dozing beside the still-wrapped presents.

I dreamt of the down comforter
Which you twined about your body,
(Accentuating the curve of your thighs)
And in the morning you fried bacon.

Waiting for the mountains' pink dawn
I recall the tiny golden hairs,
(In the small of your back)
And how they danced when you laughed.

Ellen Savage

LATE AUTUMN SUMAC

We close the door on our argument
and step into the gray-brown day
where everything is
shriveling,
      dying off,
           blowing away,
                  discarded and vacated. Walking side by side mulling
our own thoughts,
I anticipate coming to the one thing I noticed yesterday
a sumac bush with velvety berries like
vermilion chenille flames, splendid torches.

The crimson clusters bear
a sign of hope and endurance
to carry me through the barren months.
As we approach the sumac, I stay quiet.
But you warm the silence with your voice
as you proclaim the sumac's loveliness.
You tenderly cup and try to restore
the bundle that is broken over—
coaxing our first mutual yearning
to flicker in my memory
until it flares and melts all of our ice.

John Kuligowski

TO MY WIFE

The first cool breeze of fall,
your perfume brushes my nose.

You were always
my favorite season,
though first sight of you
belongs to
quintessential summer—

I remember your wet hair
beneath the Midwest sun
and understand I am
to be thirsty forever

whatever the month, the year.

Mark DeCarteret

ORIGINAL LOVE

this kissing without strategy,
yes, the ballooned lips
and trespassing tongues—
two more or less bodies
trying to reach an accordance
with the overhead light
and those sharpest of stars
yet, because we won't ever
be comfortable finding the words
to let the other one know
of our losses, our emptying lungs,
we'll remain this soft puzzle,
our arms eternally asleep

Don Russ

WITCH'S APPLES

In an Abandoned Orchard on Burningtown Creek

Witch's apples they weren't,
unplumped to that poisonous candy-red
we now expect. And deep down
I wasn't snow white.

Yet there I was, as dizzy as bees
with possibility, ready to play old scenes:
here, she said, pulling down a branch,
have one—they're organic.

Smelling the sweet decay,
treading the winey fallen flesh to mud,
I knew my death, my ecstasy.
I took a bite.

Dorothy Fryd

URBANITE

She isn't used to the country-side;
brambles paw her ankles, mosquitoes

take her blood, so he rolls down the turn-ups
of her city jeans. With the tips of his fingers,

he crushes pineapple weed for her
to smell. On the bridge, as the sky

loses its flame, they watch mayflies mating,
the rise and fall of their one-day dance.

Some of nature will remain a secret
for now: spit anaesthetizing nettle stings,

the male cicada dying on the day it learns
to love, the kinds of flowers to change scent.

They sleep under a carved-out tree, limbs
interlaced like undulating waves. Morning comes

with a chaotic wink; when the first bird is heard,
he whispers *moon, don't go, don't leave us now.*

Tommy Bui

KRISTINA

Will you twirl for me
As you did at nineteen
Under the apricot tree
Your dress was hope with green.

Rodney Nelson

KNOWN REACH

it might have been Leeds we met in
or some other city north enough
to dim at midday when a cloud
lay over
              I had said one word and
you were of utter mind to be
this summer latening time with me
             how we went
or wound up at a
South Dakota mountain I did not
have to know when I woke to your
trim nakedness
             we were already
quenched it seemed but you fed me choc-
olate cake with love and let me use
your toothbrush
             I did not have one
must not have dared to plan or to pack
even though the cabin was mine
and we had arrived in my maroon
sedan
             you were off alone to
climb the mountain which did not deso-
late me nor did I wonder why
I a trekking man had not gone too
only watched you through the window
             you had an
animal in your arms
a cat maybe not that it meant
anything
             what mattered was to load
the sedan then drive to the top
surprise you

or not in that we had
agreed without a word I would
what meant was
a love too good to be
talkative we could trust in to
lengthen a moment beyond known reach
I started
up to where I would
meet you
have not reached it yet but I
know who you were and you know me

Len Kuntz

ALADDIN

There was something once,
a small shimmering thing
that sat between us
that was us
burgeoning,
beckoning bigger than either of us knew;
but now it rests in a dim closet
no thicker than a dime,
no different than Aladdin's lamp,
waiting patiently for fingers
to bring it to life.

If you could move your heart
a little to the left,
I would slip in behind you,
spooning,
rubbing just gently enough
to let you know how much
I care.

Chuck Augello

THURSDAY NIGHT, SOMETIME IN JULY

So we found ourselves embraced;
the soft landing of our lips
an unexpected twist
to your vowed indifference
to how much we'd grown intertwined.

You closed your eyes, shades drawn tight,
but still—you blinked. You blinked,
and in the chaos of your rumpled lavender sheets
we became those words you never believed,
words you never said.

But that didn't matter, not then, not with our bodies
locked in your second-hand sunken bed, as the opera
of distant sirens and your neighbor's TV ushered us
toward morning, toward that awkward cup of coffee
and whatever the hell might happen next.

What mattered was You—
padding toward the kitchen in my old red flannel shirt,
bare feet tapping the hardwood floor
like Morse Code; symbols neither of us knew
but could both misinterpret—and so we did.

As one by one, I erased your scars
and traced them on my skin, like a map,
like an archive, like a secret formula
for keeping you near. But already you had vanished,
a warm fog I would inhabit—until my next wayward embrace.

John D. Fry

THE ULTIMATE TRUST

after Carole Maso

to let go into the lovely,
lilting world, a kind of forever

even after the brightest candle, its song
finished, finally, becomes one with the dark.

to walk this earth with you.
to hold your hand while you whisper in

my heart. *hermoso, que te quiero,*
tell me you are there, *hermoso*—

because the mica-flecked galaxy
shining in your sunlit . . .

because the light!
in your eyes . . .

I was more blind than Paul
I was more doubting than Thomas

until I touched—
so I could—

I can!
see you.

Loretta Sylvestre

WINTER DOWN, SPRING DREAMS

for BC

Sometime
In middle spring,
Having the freedom to love,
I'll lay down with you on the new-turned soil of the garden,
Just a worn-thin cotton sheet between our skins
And Earth.
We'll harvest early yields,
Gather love in basket hearts
To savor later at leisure.
Listen close,
We'll share the sound, below us, Earth's heart beating
Slow and deep, eternal.
Afterward,
Eyes open,
We'll see that it was only
The beat of butterfly wings.

Sometime
In summer new,
Having the freedom to love,
We'll find the ocean when seeking respite from the too-hot sun.
We'll go down to water's edge among shore birds,
Strip clothes
And lay them on a rock,
Colors singing in the sun,
Dancing in the breeze, our bright flag.
Our bare skins
We'll lay on cool wet sand, beneath which perhaps
Clams await the new tide.

Our love like
Ocean hands
Tender wash of blood and salt
Sleeking our skins like seal fur.

Sometime
In August blaze,
Having the freedom to love,
We'll hike the cool woods. On our backs we'll carry ripe pink peaches
And a soft-worn hand-stitched quilt. We'll know our place,
Where pines
Stand tall guard, and maples
Coax from sunlight gilded rays,
Bowls of yellow heat. Liquid light
Will dapple
Our wild skins like spotted flanks of plains horses.
We'll eat peaches, hungry.
Like horses,
Lick salt skin.
Like birds, make of love a song.
And sleep replete with peach flesh.

Sometime
September night,
Having the freedom to love,
Under a blanket of full round moon and ancient star-born light
Your smooth skin will glow silver and indigo,
Shining.
I'll trace curves, cheek, jaw, brow,
Follow the lines of your back
Into the hollow 'neath your ribs,
Glide my hands
Over shoulders and limbs, your breasts, your belly,
Cup the mounds of your ass
And pull you
Close to me.
Our bodies will share secrets
Until the sun comes for us.

Sometime
In autumn gold,
Having the freedom to love,
We'll run through chilled mist, kicking leaves around us like dancing wind.
Pelting drops of hard cold rain send tender skins
Inside
The steaming wood-warmed house.
We have too many clothes on,
We'll say, and drop them on chair backs,
Head for bed,
Spin love like leaves in wind and rain and thunder,
Autumn's darkest weather.
We'll confuse
Our own breaths
With the blowing of the storm
Outside our darkened window.

Sometime
When winter walks,
Having the freedom to love,
Sit with me, my dear, at the window as a short day's light fails
And the snow falls into night. Close the curtains.
Bring quilts
Near the hearth. Lace tea with
Damiana, sweet yellow
Honey, love potion made by bees.
We're drowsy,
But your hands have plans, find my secrets,
Draw from depth of winter
Blazing core,
Heat and light.
I will love you then as now.
You'll bank our coals for morning.

Later
When midnight's passed,
Having the freedom to love,
Burrowed in blankets, we'll sleep like she-bears, winter down, spring dreams.

Dave Migman

AMANDA

i want to know everything—your life, your breath,

unroll the canvas for me
so that I might color some forms
however long, however sweet

for as long as there is happiness and trust
and the heart-beat jungle rhythm
of love is love

to lie beneath you and
feel your claws upon me
carve your name upon
the hump of my woes

Joan McNerney

WINTER SOLSTICE

Ice blue mountains
Wind-swept skies.
There are always these...

And you, standing
silent as the sun
burning through
this day.
You are my sun,
my heaven on earth.

You bring bright ribbons,
handfuls of crystal,
to fasten my hair.

Stay with me this
long evening. I will
hide in your arms, away
from ice blue winds.
We will be warm together.

Glyn Pope

STACCATO DREAMS

I

I came into your room this morning
   wondering if you knew I was there
        laid sprawled
on the bed sleeping
hair askew
not woken by the morning sunshine

II

When I came back here
all these hundreds of miles
looked at the walls
        looked at the ceiling
   knowing that one day
we would share our dreams again

Laury A. Egan

ETERNITY

Though now
the moon is waxing,
pressing its yellow crescent
into the dark lavender sky,
alas, the nights grow shorter,
though for us we wish
them longer, as they were
when we met in late November.

Dearest, there will never be time
enough to love you, to show you
all the places you reside in my heart.
If we lived for a hundred,
for a thousand years, I would regret
I had not told you, had not
shown you, everything I feel.

Leila A. Fortier

ORCHESTRA OF YOUR NAME

Can you hear the rain? This is what you do to me ~ This is what you have
Made of me~ My infinite tears streaming ~ Paired with my
Countless heart's beating ~ Simultaneously
Splayed ~ In watercolor splash
And rolling waves ~
Immaculately
Unfettered
Is the
Span
Of
My
Love
~ For you ~
Dancing in
Delirium to your lost that
I have found ~ Where even the stars
Have come unbound ~ To the orchestra of your name

Emily Severance

ON THE EDGE OF A BEAM

(Yuanyang County, China)

Spring again. Open the windows
so the red-rumped swallows
can resurrect last year's nest;
press their hearts against our ceiling.

Leave the casements open
so flights in and out
bless our cliff-balanced home.

As they collect beaks of paddy
mud to mold a mating bed,
we'll plant terraces of rice,
bend backs, wave rears,
join their red-rump dives.

Cheri L.R. Taylor

ARC OF A DANCE

How many times have we stepped away?

> two-four timing
> a metronome of hands

hold and release
more capture than caress

> forward movement
> a sunlight backdrop
> the pin-pointed center
> of the pupil

I see your soul.

> we play the music of denial
> terrified it will stop
> and we'll have to go back
> to walking

even getting the steps wrong
allows us time
in each other's arms

> what you can't give
> resting on the tip of your tongue
> in the breath you can't draw in
> or push out

Let it play.

>   our thoughts on a turn table
>   scratching out the verses
>   a constant excruciating spin

the taste of you
a song
I can't get out of my head

Jean Brasseur

PARALLEL EXISTENCE

Where longing is the answer, not the question.

full moon
milky yellow
sketches shadows

Dressed in shadows with bare feet silent, crossing sand. We shed words like extra skin.

voyeurs
watch from trees
owls and opossums

Silver shimmers skim the surface. Limbs drift amongst one another.

tiny wave
pulls a pebble
under its wing

Dawn sprays pink mist across the lake, brushes swans floating tandem.

I dream us
this way.

David L. O'Neal

SHADOWS

Do shadows of former lovers
flitter in the corners of your mind's eye
like floaters in your field of vision?
If they are your lovers, I don't care.
I love you.
If they are mine, they are phantoms,
bland bleached bones
dissolving evermore into dust,
diminishing at every moment,
little specks of disappearing memory.
Don't let these tiny shades make you uneasy
…
I want to die while you still love me.

Richard T. Rauch

AMONG THE GLORIES

We walk alone again among the glories,
amid the splendors of lavender, trading
dreams in the vibrancy of the morning air.—

You will pause to pick one. You always do—
only one—bending at the waist, your form
articulating through light cotton

with the motion of your grace, a flower
animalized among flowers, rising
with the one you've chosen, crushing it,

taking in its sweet essence hungrily.
You'll throw back your hair and smile lavishly,
mocking the multitudes with your laughter.

And so it is among the glories I'll stay—held
by your smirk, that way you wrinkle your nose, laughing
at me still—trading dreams with you, alone.

Elizabeth Ashe

WITHOUT TITLES

I love you everyday.
I would say this with my hands
so that even you, would stay.

Such words we don't need to convey.
Hands on hips, quiz of a walk backwards, stand.
I love you. Every day

I mumble in the air, to relay
it with inked fingers, art spilt across a page, bland
stains on the tongue—
so that even you, would stay.

Something akin to life. Sometimes I play
a mix, a gift without titles, letters grandly
I love you. "Everyday"

is the Sharpie-marked line. To say
it again slips in beside my making dinner plans
so that's even. You would stay.

Change of venue, the light may
want a different painting, walls crammed
at eye level.
I love you everyday.
So that even you, would stay.

Luke Maguire Armstrong

POUR VERA

Truth is the flower
That blooms in my night
Long is the hour it
Germinates before light.

Vera, there are a million things a poem could say.
But it's really never about what the poem says,
But who we say them to and why.
And this poem I'm writing to you, the truth that has
Flowered in my life.
I come to you not with gifts in hand,
But in heart, in my desire for your bliss.

I give you the moon, but only when you
Are startled to see it shining in that unknown
Heaven beyond Earth. Please take it only
When the night seems darker than you can bear.
Take it when it seems the only thing left that is
Constant, the only thing that has not fallen from the sky.

I give you not the sunrise, but the certainty that
Night will always be conquered by the humble
First light of dawn. Please take it quietly and with tea.
Find warmth in it during the cool bite of the dawn, and
Remember that this gift will return every morning until forever.

I give you the innocent laughter of children, the kind
That reminds us that to fully grow up is to stop living.

In this laughter is all anyone ever needs to remember
In order to not forget why we smile, why we love,
Why happiness can overflow from rivers we
Once thought had dried up.

I give you the hope for your happiness on this special day.
I give you my hope that you smile, that you laugh, that as
You stand, where all of us do,
Coming from this and going to that,
I hope your road is
Filled with joy, hopes, dreams, and my hugs and kisses.
I love you, please always be kind to yourself.

V. Ulea

DREAMS

for Vadim

Dreams are what always bring us near
While daily life stubbornly estranges us.
I watch you sleeping in your astral sphere
Washed by the streams of Aquarius.
Comets lighten your dreams on their flight,
Mixing "beneath" and "above."
You never search for the meaning of life,
But only for the meaning of love.
Dreams are swaying us in their cradle.
Until dawn, we will ride their chaise.
It was them who once brought us together.
It was us who once gave them that chance.

JoAnne Blackwelder

ON SURPRISING YOU

I want you just so, painted there,
turning your face up to me,
alight beneath sun-sandy hair:

Vermeer-gold profile, Holbein nose,
Sir Thomas More black eyes that hold
me everywhere, as soils enclose

their morning rain; your shirt a Rembrandt
cotton brightfall from your shoulders
to your hands. There, as you stand,

clouding perspective in this light,
I cannot paint you, but aware
how briefly grace will touch my sight,

I welcome to my heart these dyes
shading the you that I will keep
on the dark side of my eyes.

Lynn Hoffman

THE TRUTH ABOUT LOVE

First you feel love; hot, adhesive.
Later you choose love; cooler,
more like gears than glue.

Choose long enough and
some day Love just becomes you
and you can just be Love.

Later, if Love doesn't want to kill you
(or even if it does)
you don't have to choose it or feel it again
any more than you have
to choose
or feel
the length of your eyes
or the color of your feet.
You are the Love and Love—
(perhaps to its dismay)—
is you.

One other thing:
if someday you stop loving in order to save your life,
if you choke off the feelings and choose something else,
Love stays with you.

After all, it's got nowhere else to go
and you can't leave the goddamn thing
at a rest stop on the Pennsylvania Turnpike
and drive off to Pittsburgh, can you?
No.

For if you try, you'd just find the sonofabitch
waiting for you at the New Stanton rest stop
drinking coffee spiked with phenobarbitol
and complaining about all the time Love
spent alone in the rain
and how the rain has ruined Love's hair.

How would you feel about choosing that?

ABOUT THE POETS

MURRAY ALFREDSON: Murray Alfredson is a retired librarian, lecturer, and a Buddhist Associate to the Multi-faith Chaplaincy Service at Flinders University of South Australia. He has published essays on meditation and inter-faith relations in *Theravada, The Middle Way, In the Round,* and *Eremos*; and he has published poems and translations in *Overland, Eremos, Ocean, Pan Gaia, Shalla, Cadenza, Orbis, Reach, Manifold, Dawn Treader, Touch Poetry,* and other journals and anthologies in Australia, the United States, and the United Kingdom. His collection, *Nectar and Light,* appeared early in 2007 in a shared volume, *Friendly Street New Poets, Volumn 12.* He was awarded the High Beam Poetry Prize in 2004 and the Poetry Unhinged Multicultural prize in 2006. His collection, *Trees on the Slope,* is in preparation. He lives on the Fleurieu Peninsula in South Australia, by Gulf St Vincent.

LUKE MAGUIRE ARMSTRONG: After college Luke Maguire Armstrong did the most financially irresponsible thing he could think of—he took out a last-minute student loan and decided to hitch-hike from Chile to Alaska. He currently lives in Antigua, Guatemala, where he directs the humanitarian development organization Nuestros Ahijados in a mission to "break the bitter chains of poverty through education and formation." This work has been featured on ABC News' "Global Health Special" and covered in dozens of other mainstream media outlets. He is the curator of humor page www.RabbleRouseTheWorld.com, author of *iPoems for the Dolphins to Click Home About,* and contributing editor to the online travel magazine TheExpeditioner.com and the offbeat travel book *The Expeditioner's Guide to the World.*

ELIZABETH ASHE: Elizabeth Ashe received an MFA in Creative Writing from Chatham University and is a MFA candidate at the Maryland Institute College of Art. In essence, Ashe is a nomadic sculptor-poet who bakes a wicked chocolate cake. She is interested in new narratives which resound like the oral tradition. She was an assistant editor for *Fourth River* and continues to edit on a freelance basis. Ashe's work has been previously published by *4Culture, Insert Content, The Synergy Project, No Teeth, The Legendary, Glass: A Literary Journal, Battered Suitcase, Dot Dot Dash,* and *Flycatcher,* among others. www.elizabethashe.com

CHUCK AUGELLO: Chuck Augello lives in New Jersey with his wife, dog, three cats, and several unnamed birds that inhabit the back yard. His poetry and fiction have appeared in *Rattle, Word Riot, Pure Francis, Hobart, decomP, Psychic Meatloaf, Muse and Stone,* and other journals.

ISAAC JAMES BAKER: Isaac James Baker lives and writes in Washington, D.C., where he is working on a master's degree in Writing from Johns Hopkins University. His short stories, poems, essays, and reporting have appeared in a wide array of publications. For more information, visit www.isaacjamesbaker.com or follow his blog at http://isaacjamesbaker.blogspot.com.

KAYLA BASHE: Kayla Bashe is a student from New Jersey. Her work has appeared in *YARN* and is upcoming in the Alpha Alumni anthology. She recently attended the Alpha SF/F/H Workshop for Young Writers. In addition to writing, Kayla enjoys musical theater and curating the extraordinary. Find her at http://twitter.com/KaylaBashe.

ANNE BASTOW: Anne Bastow graduated from the University of Arizona with a degree in English Literature. She has worked as an online magazine editor, communications manager, and freelance writer. She lives in her hometown on the eastern side of northern Michigan where she continues to pursue the poetic life.

GARY BECK: Gary Beck has spent most of his adult life as a theater director and worked as an art dealer when he couldn't earn a living in the theater. His chapbook *Remembrance* was published by Origami Condom Press and *The Conquest of Somalia* was published by Cervena Barva Press. A collection of his poetry, *Days of Destruction*, was published by Skive Press. His poetry collection *Expectations* was published by Rogue Scholars Press. His plays and translations of Moliere, Aristophanes, and Sophocles were produced Off Broadway and his poetry has appeared in numerous literary magazines.

ROXANNA BENNETT: Roxanna Bennett is a Canadian writer who divided her childhood between Toronto, Ontario, and Corner Brook, Newfoundland. Currently she lives and works in Toronto as a writer and artist educator and is one of the poetry editors at *Halfway Down the Stairs*. Her poetry has appeared in such publications as *The Fiddlehead*, *The Dalhousie Review*, *The Antigonish Review*, *CV2*, *Slice Magazine*, *Popshot*, and *Descant*. Her nonfiction work can be found at *Feminists for Choice*, *Gender Focus*, *Hip Mama*, *Used Furniture Review*, and *40 Moms Club*.

JUSTIN BLACKBURN: Justin Blackburn loves writing. He has had hundreds of poems published in various journals, anthologies, magazines, and 'zines. His chapbook, *Farting Fire*, is the best seller at Virgogray Press. He recently finished a novel titled *The Upper Middle Class Suburban White Boy Enlightened Guru Blues*. He is convinced this book will raise the vibration of everyone who reads it. Find out more about Justin Blackburn at www.justinblackburnlovesyou.com

JOANNE BLACKWELDER: For many years, JoAnne Blackwelder worked in publishing, typesetting, and printing in New York. She also tried a few other jobs, like automotive parts cataloguing and real estate sales. She owned her own printing company in Manhattan for more than ten years. All of this activity to pay the mortgage and the college bills—while simultaneously renovating a brownstone, supporting her husband's screenplay and novel writing, and bringing up two daughters—was stressful, but music and poetry kept her sane. Now retired and living in Ocean City, New Jersey, JoAnne works as an organist and choir director. She has written poetry since childhood, and her poems have appeared in *The Formalist, The Lyric, Poet's Review, The East Hampton Newsletter*, and *Printing News*.

LOUISE BLAYDON: Louise Blaydon is a rock-climber, an academic, and a writer of erotic fiction, but before she was any of these things, she was a poet. Her professional poetic endeavors have mostly been confined to the sphere of editing to date, but she hopes to change this soon. https://sites.google.com/site/louiseblaydon/

JENNIFER HOLLIE BOWLES: Jennifer Hollie Bowles lives, writes, edits, and publishes literature in Oak Ridge, Tennessee. Her third chapbook, *Suck My Clit Freud*, is forthcoming with SAM Publishing. She always seeks the marrow underneath (www.themedullareview. com), but after years spent creating through the catalyst of trauma, she has recently found her poetic voice playing in the light.

JEAN BRASSEUR: Jean Brasseur lives and writes in Northern Virginia. She does not have an MFA, nor does she teach writing (other than volunteering with elementary students). This has not stopped her from pursuing a lifelong love affair with reading and writing poetry. Her work has appeared in *The Battered Suitcase, gutter eloquence, Phantom Kangaroo,* and others.

TOMMY BUI: Tommy Bui is prone to concise confabulations and off-kilter katzenjammers. Growing up in soporific small-town Los Angeles, he was quick to cast off the bowlines and traverse the world. His travels have taken him from the bonnie bucolic bryns of Wales to the vast and desolate steppes of Kazakhstan. Tommy will admit to being interested in antique timepieces, scrimshaw, and obscure cheeses. But he will staunchly deny an interest in McRibs, café racers, and Metal Gear Solid. He hopes to score a decisive goal for England in the World Cup some day. Tommy holds a master's degree in English Literature and is a returned Peace Corps volunteer who served in Central Asia. Many can attest that he is mostly underwhelming.

STEPHEN BUSBY: Stephen Busby is a traveller, writer, and photographer based in the Findhorn Community, northern Scotland. His prose and poetry have appeared in *Cezanne's Carrot*, *r.kv.r.y*, *Slow Trains*, *The Battered Suitcase*, *Santa Fe Writers Project*, *Visionary Tongue*, and *Secret Attic*. He runs workshops and events on transformational healing themes in various countries, and you can find him online at www.deepsystemshealing.com/stephen

JOHN BYRNE: John Byrne lives in Albany, Oregon with Cheryl French, the woman who inspired the sonnet, and their daughter. He writes short plays, short stories, and short—mostly formal—poems. His work appears frequently in print and Internet journals and has been staged in Washington, Oregon, and Missouri.

TINA V. CABRERA: Tina V. Cabrera earned her MFA in Creative Writing from San Diego State University in 2009. Excerpts from her novel, short fiction, and poetry have appeared in journals such as *Midwest Literary Magazine*, *Outrider Press/TallGrass Writers*, *Fiction International*, *City Works*, and *The San Diego Poetry Annual*. She teaches writing at local colleges in San Diego. She will recite prose and poetry in exchange for stimulating conversation and a cup of coffee. Visit her writer's blog at http://cannyuncanny.wordpress.com/.

TETMAN CALLIS: Tetman Callis is a writer and artist who lives in Albuquerque, New Mexico. His stories and poems have appeared in various publications, including *The New York Tyrant*, *Neon*, *Ontario Review*, *Denver Quarterly*, and *Cutthroat*. Many of these published works are available on his website at www.tetmancallis.com. He holds a bachelor's degree in Philosophy, with high honors, from the University of Texas at El Paso, studied Creative Writing with Gordon Lish in New York City and at the MFA program at the University of New Mexico, and makes his living as a legal assistant.

JAKE DAVID: Jake David is a thinker living outside Massena, New York. While not a traditionally published author, his work has been published in *The Battered Suitcase, Seahorse Rodeo Folk Review, ken*again*, and *ditch*. His debut novel, *A Symphony* is scheduled for release mid-2012. When not writing, he can be found performing at open mic events around Ontario, Canada.

MARK DECARTERET: Mark DeCarteret's work has appeared in the anthologies *American Poetry: The Next Generation* (Carnegie Mellon Press), *Brevity & Echo: Short Short Stories by Emerson College Alums* (Rose Metal Press), *Thus Spake the Corpse: An Exquisite Corpse Reader* (Black Sparrow Press), and *Under the Legislature of Stars—62 New Hampshire Poets* (Oyster River Press), which he also co-edited. *Flap*, his fifth book, was published by Finishing Line Press in 2011.

LAURA DENNIS: Laura Dennis has been published in the anthology *Home and Away from House of Blue Skies* and other online venues. She has two chapbooks titled *Wheels on the Bus* and *The Bookshelf*. She lives in Edmonton, Alberta Canada, with her husband. https://www.facebook.com/pages/Laura-Dennis-Poet/134363053288750?sk=info

ANTHONY DIMATTEO: Anthony DiMatteo's poetry has been featured in recent or forthcoming issues of *Avatar Review, Connotation Press, Cordite Poetry Review, Denver Syntax, Front Porch, Long Island Quarterly, Main Street Rag*, and *Tar River Poetry*. *Smartish Pace* awarded one poem first place in an annual contest for 2010, nominating it for a Pushcart Prize. This poem "In Need of Asking" is from his book of poems *Beautiful Problems*. To a dead man, any problem would be beautiful. The state of non-being is what "strawman" in the poem's last line anticipates. He invites you to leave a trace at his campsite: www.anthonydimatteo.wordpress.com.

LIZ DOLAN: Liz Dolan's second poetry manuscript, *A Secret of Long Life*, which is seeking a publisher, was nominated for the Robert McGovern Prize.Her first poetry collection, *They Abide*, was published by March Street Press. A five-time Pushcart Prize nominee and winner of The Best of the Web, she has also won a $6,000 established artist fellowship in poetry and two honorable mentions in prose from the Delaware Division of the Arts. She recently won $250 for prose from *The Nassau Review*. Her nine grandkids live one block away from her. They pepper her life.

JAMES H. DUNCAN: James H. Duncan is a tramp, a gentleman, a poet, a dreamer, a lonely fellow, always hopeful of romance and adventure. James is a magazine editor and freelance writer living in New York City, and he is the founder of *Hobo Camp Review*, an online literary 'zine dedicated to the traveling word. Twice nominated for the Best of the Net, his poetry and short stories have found homes in dozens of publications, including *Pulp Modern, Underground Voices*, and *Poetry Salzberg Review*. http://jameshduncan.blogspot.com.

DANIEL EAST: Daniel East is an Australian writer currently residing in Sydney. His poetry and non-fiction have appeared in *Cordite, Mascara, Red River Review,* and *Voiceworks,* and his play *Sexy Tales of Paleontology* (co-written with Patrick Lenton) won the 2010 Sydney Fringe comedy award. He is also one of four surviving members of Australia's only performance poetry boy band, The Bracket Creeps.

LAURY A. EGAN: Laury A. Egan's two poetry collections, *Snow, Shadows, a Stranger* and *Beneath the Lion's Paw*, were published by FootHills. Two books, *Jenny Kidd,* a psychological suspense novel (Vagabondage Press), and *Fog and Other Stories* (StoneGarden.net Publishing), will be released in 2012. www.lauryaegan.com

DANIEL J. FITZGERALD: Dan Fitzgerald started writing a number of years ago. It has only been recently that he has tried to be published. He worked a long time in the print field until technology took those jobs away. He resides in Pontiac, Illinois, working in the meat and bakery departments of a local grocer. He is hoping they open a candle section to further his career. Some of the magazines and journals he has been published in are *Poetalk, Nomads Choir, Writers' Journal,* and *The Advocate*. He can be contacted at dfitz467@yahoo.com.

LEILA A. FORTIER: Leila A. Fortier is a writer, artist, poet, and photographer currently residing on Okinawa, Japan. Her poetry is a unique hybrid form in which her words are specially crafted into abstract visual designs. Much of her work has been translated into French, Italian, Spanish, Arabic, German, Hindi, and Japanese. Her work has been published in a vast array of literary magazines, journals, and reviews both in print and online. She has appeared in several books, anthologies, and freelance publications. In 2007, she initiated the anthology *A World of Love: Voices for Carmen* as a benefit against domestic violence, and in 2010 composed a photo book titled *Pappankalan, India: Through the Eyes of Children* to benefit the education of impoverished Indian children. She is also the author of *Metanoia's Revelation* through *iUniverse*. A complete listing of her published works can be found at: www.leilafortier.com

MANDA FREDERICK: Manda Frederick holds an MFA in Creative Nonfiction from the Inland Northwest Center for Writers and a master's degree in Literary Studies from Western Washington University. She has published nonfiction in the *White Whale Review* and *Switchback* magazine. Her essay "The Saw Tooth" was a finalist published for *Adventum Magazine's* 2011 Ridge to River contest. She has poetry forthcoming in *Muse & Stone*, and her poems recently appeared in *Stirring* and the *Iron Horse Literary Review*. She is the winner of the 2011 Press 53 Open Award for poetry. Her fiction appeared in *Four Paper Letters*, and she has an interview with poet Robert Wrigley forthcoming in the *Bellingham Review*. She is currently an assistant professor of writing arts at Rowan University in New Jersey.

SUSAN FREE: Susan Free is a freelance writer and lover of books. She lives online at http://susansbooklove.blogspot.com.

JOHN D. FRY: John D. Fry grew up in west and south Texas and attended Davidson College in Davidson, North Carolina where he received a bachelor's degree in English. He is currently an MFA candidate in Poetry at Texas State University. His poems have appeared in *Blood Orange Review, Bare Root Review, St. Sebastian Review,* and *BorderSenses* and are forthcoming in *The Texas Review, Konundrum Engine Literary Review,* and *New Border,* an anthology to be published by Texas A&M University Press,. He lives in San Antonio, Texas.

DOROTHY FRYD: Dorothy Fryd resides in the South of England where she teaches Creative Writing at Kent University and co-tutors for The Barbican Young Poets Project. Her work has been published in magazines such as *The Rialto, BRAND Literary Magazine, South Bank Poetry Magazine, Aesthetica Magazine,* and *The Interpreter's House.* Her forthcoming collection *Turbulence* will be published with Flipped Eye in 2012. www.dorothyfryd.co.uk

ALAN GANN: Most of Alan Gann's friends are surprised to find he is still at large and allowed to teach creative writing workshops in at-risk schools, and sex ed at a Unitarian Universalist church. He is on the board of the Dallas Poets Community and is a poetry editor for their literary journal, *Illya's Honey.* Somehow, he still finds time to ride his bike, wander in the woods, look at birds, and photograph dragonflies. Recently, his poems have appeared in *Sentence, Main Street Rag, Borderlands, Sojourn,* and the *Texas Poetry Calendar.* In 2011, Alan had poems nominated for a Pushcart Prize by *Red River Review* and a Best of the Net award by Red Fez.

CHAITALI DEEPAK GAWADE: Chaitali Deepak Gawade is a content writer for an online publishing house by day. At night, she is an aspiring writer fuelled by tea and coffee.

BRIGITTE GOETZE: Brigitte Goetze, biologist, goat farmer, and writer, lives in the foothills of Oregon 's Coast Range. She has been published by *Oregon Humanities, Quiet Mountain Essays, Outwardlink, Four and Twenty, Calyx, Women Artists Datebook 2011, Mused, Imitation Fruit, Gold Man Review,* and others. A chapbook, titled *Rose Hips,* is available from the author.

PETER J. GRIECO: Peter J. Grieco is a former school bus driver who has taught American Literature and Culture in Ankara and Seoul. Recent publications include poems in *Subliminal Interiors, Psychic Meatloaf, Infinity's Kitchen, Turbulence, Post Poetry, Dear Sir, New Writing, Heavy Hands, Black Heart, House Organ*, and *Indefinite Space*. He is currently studying mathematics and French in Buffalo, New York, his native city.

SARA HARMAN-CLARKE: Sara Harman-Clarke is a freelance writer and student living in Brighton, on the south coast of England. An enthusiastic writer from a young age, Sara is currently studying for a master's degree in Creative and Critical Writing at Sussex University, having completed her undergraduate degree in English Literature and Language. Poetry and short fictions are Sara's main focus at present. "Little Love" is her first published poem, a great encouragement for Sara, who aspires to publish her own anthology of poetry. She has recently branched out into writing reviews and articles for magazines and online websites. Read more of Sara's work at www.saraharmanclarke.wordpress.com.

H. EDGAR HIX: H. Edgar Hix grew up in a small city, then in the country, in the American South. Hix has spent most of his adulthood in the North, in Minneapolis, Minnesota. Hix has held a variety of jobs: warehouseman, library clerk, legal secretary, call center representative, and system analyst. Hix has been publishing poetry and other types of writing, for some 40 years. He finally got a college degree in his late 40s. He figures he's got some kind of record: He completed first semester of Freshman's Comp in 1972 and the second semester of Freshman's Comp in 2001. Hix lives with his wife, seven cats and one dog, who suffers the cats with (usually) quiet dignity. Hix has published nearly 500 poems, several essays and articles, a children's book (way back in 1980), a poetry chapbook, and other miscellaneous things.

JOHN OLIVER HODGES: John Oliver Hodges walks the streets of Flushing, New York, where he often holds his opened bag of potato chips out to strangers he passes. "Would you like a chip?"

he asks. If it happens to be raining, he will creep up beside you and hold his umbrella over your head. He has received much laughter for such behavior, and so far, nobody has socked him in the face—knock on wood! His poetry has appeared previously in *The Southern Poetry Anthology, Steam Ticket*, and *Rattle,* and can be viewed online at *Hell Gate Review, Gutter Eloquence, My Favorite Bullet*, and *Frigg*. His novella, titled *War of the Crazies* is available from Main Street Rag.

LYNN HOFFMAN: Lynn Hoffman is a novelist and food writer who lives in Philadelphia. He has a daughter named Spencer, and he'd love to tell you how well she's doing. He's been a chef, a professor of culinary arts, a merchant seaman, and a cab driver. He hopes to have a regular job one day. His latest book is *The Short Course in Beer*, from Arcade Books. drfood55@gmail.com

A. J. HUFFMAN: A. J. Huffman is a poet and freelance writer in Daytona Beach, Florida. She has previously published three collections of poetry: *The Difference Between Shadows and Stars, Carrying Yesterday*, and *Cognitive Distortion*. She has also published her work in national and international literary journals such as *Avon Literary Intelligencer, Writer's Gazette*, and *The Penwood Review*. Find more about A. J. Huffman, including additional information and links to her work at http://www.facebook.com/profile. php?id=100000191382454 and http://twitter.com/#!/poetess222 .

C. V. HUNT: C. V. Hunt is the author of the *Endlessly* series, *Danse Macabre*, and various other works. Her writing usually contains elements of horror, dark fantasy, paranormal, and the bizarre. C.V. also writes book reviews for *The LL Book Review*, and in her spare time, she enjoys reading, writing, painting, and listening to a variety of music. You can find out more about her writing by visiting her website at www.authorcvhunt.com

LISA JAYNE: Lisa Jayne was born and grew up in Essex, in the southeast of England. After completing art college, she worked as a library assistant by day and explored London's subcultures by night;

dancing in fetish clubs, following bands, and modelling for artists. Although a prolific and passionate painter, she rejected the standard commercial route to success, and in her late twenties moved to Brighton, where she began writing as well as painting, preferring the raw emotion and instant reaction of a poetry reading to the tedious engineering of an art exhibition. Lisa Jayne likes to sleep. Her work can be found at www.lisajaynewritings.blogspot.com.

MICHAEL LEE JOHNSON: Michael Lee Johnson, published in 25 countries, is a poet and freelance writer from Itasca, Illinois, who lived in exile in Edmonton, Alberta Canada for ten years during the Vietnam War. His new poetry chapbook, *From Which Place the Morning Rises*, and his new photo version of *The Lost American: from Exile to Freedom* and chapbooks are available at http://www.lulu.com/spotlight/promomanusa; with a new chapbooks and *Challenge of Night and Day*, and *Chicago Poems*: http://www.lulu.com/product/paperback/challenge-of-night-and-day-and-chicago-poems-(night)/12443733

DAVID W. JONES: David W. Jones is an American poet, writer of narrative fiction, and avid blogger. His passion is creating literary expressions involving the life of a dreamer challenged by the tyranny of reality. David began writing poetry in December 2009 on his award-winning blog site *1MereMortal - Dealing With This Thing Called Life* (http://1MereMortal.me), as well as posting his poetry and narrative writings on various community blog sites. In November 2010, his poem "Stained Glass" was published in a monthly showcase of poets across the Internet called *Poetic License*. When he is not writing, David enjoys reading suspense thriller novels, playing video games, and collecting comic books.

AUNIA KAHN: Aunia Kahn is a writer, poet, and published author of the *Silver Era Tarot* deck and *Obvious Remote Chaos*, a book of lyrics, poetry, and photography. Her forthcoming works include: *Inspirations for Survivors* deck, the *Lowbrow Tarot* book and tarot deck as well as a follow-up to *Obvious Remote Chaos, Minding the*

Sea: Inviting the Muses over for Tea. Kahn's multitalented avenues of expression are not limited to the written word as her internationally recognized career as an artist also attests. Find Aunia and links to all her projects and galleries of work at www.auniakahn.com.

JOHN KULIGOWSKI: John Kuligowski currently lives in the Midwest. His poetry and short stories have appeared most recently in *Word Riot*, *The Molotov Cocktail*, the anthology *Unlikely Stories of the Third Kind*, and *Gloom Cupboard*. He has an abiding fixation with semiotics and is currently at work on a novel.

LEN KUNTZ: Len Kuntz is a writer from Washington State. Nominated for The Pushcart Prize and other awards, his work appears widely in print and online at such journals as *Boston Literary Magazine*, *Lower Eastside Review*, *Pank*, and others. Every few days, he shares his thoughts about life at lenkuntz.blogspot.com

MAUDE LARKE : Maude Larke lives in Dijon, France. She has come back to her own writing after a career in the American, English and French university systems, analyzing others' texts and films. She has also returned to the classical music world as an ardent amateur after fifteen years of piano and voice in her youth. She has several short stories and poems, three novels, and two screenplays to offer so far. Publications include *Naugatuck River Review*, *Cyclamens and Swords*, *riverbabble*, *Doorknobs and BodyPaint*, *Sketchbook*, *Cliterature*, *Short, Fast, and Deadly*, and *The Centrifugal Eye*.

CHRISTINA LOVIN: Christina Lovin is the author of *What We Burned for Warmth* and *Little Fires*. A two-time Pushcart Prize nominee and multi-award winner, her writing has appeared in numerous journals and anthologies. Having served as Writer-in-Residence at Devil's Tower National Monument and Andrews Forest in Oregon, she served as inaugural Writer-in-Residence at Connemara, the last home of Carl Sandburg. Lovin has been a resident fellow at Virginia Center for the Creative Arts, Vermont Studio Center, Prairie Center of the Arts, Orcas Island Artsmith, and

Footpaths House in the Azores. Her work has been supported with grants from Elizabeth George Foundation, Kentucky Foundation for Women, and Kentucky Arts Council. She resides with four dogs in a rural central Kentucky. More information: www.christinalovin.com

ANDREW J. LUCAS: Andrew Lucas was born in England and emigrated to Canada at the tender age of four. He grew up in the scenic Okanagan region of British Columbia, which influences many of the images and textures of his poetry. In 1986, he won the Okanagan College Poetry Contest and has had a number of poem published over the years. His style is reminiscent of a young Al Prudy, appealing to the senses of the reader. He is also active in the pen and paper roleplaying game industry and has had a number of solo books produced by various publishers. Presently, he is working on an original RPG book revolving around a far future colonization mission which goes horribly wrong.

KATIE MANNING: Katie Manning is Editor-in-Chief of *Rougarou* and a doctoral fellow in English at UL-Lafayette. Her writing has been published in *New Letters, PANK, Poet Lore, So to Speak,* and *The Sow's Ear Poetry Journal*, among other journals and anthologies, and she is the 2011 winner of *The Nassau Review's* Author Award for Poetry.

DOUG MATHEWSON: Doug Mathewson is a writer who spent his formative years turning over brook stones, looking for new friends, or a means of escape. As a writer, he is best known for his for his painting and mixed-media sculptures. The art world has been unimpressed with the exception of his *Head-of-Goliath-a-Day* Series. Since 1937, he has created daily a self portrait using the famous image of young David with the severed head of the giant Goliath. The more famous pictures portray men or women from all ages and walks of life as David. Some days they are robots, space squids, media pop-stars, or household objects. The artist is always the head. Gratefully, none of this can be seen at Full of Crow Press and Distribution where he is a collaborator or at *Blink-Ink* which he edits.

BRADLEY MCILWAIN: Bradley McIlwain is a Canadian-based writer and poet who lives and works in rural Ontario as a freelance reporter, covering stories on local heritage, the arts, and human interest. The narratives in his poetry often stem from a desire to paint the natural world around him and exploring its intimate connection with memory. In addition to the classics, he enjoys reading the work of M.G. Vassanji, Gregory Scofield, and Tom MacGregor. He holds a bachelor's degree, Honours, from Trent University, with a major in English Literature. His first book of poems, *Fracture*, was printed in the summer of 2010. For more information on *Fracture* and Bradley's poetry, you are encouraged to visit him at www.bradleymcilwain. blogspot.com

NATALIE MCNABB: Natalie McNabb lives and writes in Washington State, where her dog and cat frolic beneath the trees of her Eden after squirrel tails, exhumed moles, and up-flung mice. She loves the color red—red dragonflies resting on bamboo stakes, red wine in her glass, red flip-flops on her red-toe-nailed feet—and words that caress, tickle, irritate, or beat against her soul. Natalie's writing appears in *Norton's Hint Fiction* and various literary publications. She has also been shortlisted for The Micro Award, Glass Woman Prize, Fish Short Story Competition and a few other contests. Please visit her at www.NatalieMcNabb.com.

JOAN MCNERNEY: Joan McNerney, originally from Brooklyn, now resides in Ravena, a town outside Albany, New York. She received her bachelor's degree in English from the Board of Regents, New York State Excelsior University. Most of her professional background was spent in the advertising business. Her poetry has been included in numerous literary magazines such as *Seven Circle Press, Dinner with the Muse, Blueline, 63 channels, Spectrum*, and three Bright Spring Press anthologies. In 2011, she received two Best of the Net nominations. Four of her books were published by fine small literary presses. She has recited her work at the National Arts Club, Russell Sage College, McNay Art Institute and other distinguished venues. A recent reading was sponsored by the American Academy of Poetry.

DAVE MIGMAN: Dave Migman is a writer and artist from Edinburgh, United Kingdom. His work has appeared in numerous poetry 'zines including *Blaze Vox, Media Virus*, and *Foliate Oak*. His novel, *The Wolf Stepped Out*, is published by Doghorn Publishing.

SUSAN MILCHMAN: Susan Milchman is a Bikram Yoga Instructor, cheese addict, and full-time animal lover. She believes that poetry is "absolute truth" in a world that is increasingly "manufactured." She considers herself an eternal student of The Loft Literary Center in Minneapolis, where she lives with her husband and two spirited daughters. Her work has been published in *Slow Trains Literary Journal, The Smoking Poet*, and *Oak Bend Review* and you can find her online at www.susanmilchman.com

CAROLINE MISNER: Caroline Misner was born in a country that at the time was known as Czechoslovakia. She immigrated to Canada in the summer of 1969. Her work has appeared in numerous consumer and literary journals in Canada, the United States, and the United Kingdom. Her short story "Strange Fruit" was nominated for the Writers' Trust/McClelland-Steward Journey Anthology Prize in 2008. In the autumn of 2010, her poem "Piano Lesson" was nominated for The Pushcart Prize and her short story "A Necessary Sadness" was nominated for a Pushcart in 2011. Her novelette, *The Watchmaker*, was published by Vagabondage Press in December 2011. Her new website is finally online: www.carolinemisner.com

ROBERT B. MORELAND: Robert Moreland has a doctorate in biochemistry and works in biomedical/clinical research. He has published poems in *Verse Wisconsin, The South Dakota Review, Towards the Light, Rope and Wire,* and several anthologies. He has coauthored two books of poems. Bob resides with his wife Rebecca in Carol Beach near Lake Michigan in Pleasant Prairie, Wisconsin.

SHARON LASK MUNSON: Sharon Lask Munson grew up in Detroit, Michigan. She attended Michigan State University and Wayne State University. She taught for the Department of Defense in schools in England, Germany, Okinawa, and Puerto Rico. After overseas teaching, Sharon drove her blue Oldsmobile up the Alcan Highway to Anchorage, Alaska where she put down new roots, taught school, married, and lived for the next twenty years. She is now retired and lives with her husband, Keith, in Eugene, Oregon. She has poems in many literary journals and anthologies. Her chapbook, *Stillness Settles Down the Lane* was published in summer 2010 by Utterred Chaos Press. *That Certain Blue*, published by Blue Light Press in 2012, is her first full-length book of poems.

NIKESH MURALI: Nikesh Murali's work (which includes comics, poems, and short stories) has appeared in more than 80 publications worldwide. His poems have been translated into Spanish, Italian, Portuguese, and French. He won the Commonwealth Short Story Prize for the Asian region in 2011. His poetry was nominated for the Pushcart Prize in 2007. He has completed his master's degree in Journalism from Griffith University, for which he was awarded the Griffith University Award for Academic Excellence in 2005, and his master's degree in Teaching from James Cook University and a bachelor's degree in English Literature and World History from University of Kerala. He is working toward his doctorate in Creative Writing. He can be found online at www.nikeshmurali.net.

RODNEY NELSON: Rodney Nelson's work began appearing in mainstream journals long ago, but he turned to fiction and did not write a poem for twenty-two years, restarting in the 2000s. So he is both older and "new." He has worked as a copy editor in the Southwest and now lives in his native northern Great Plains. See his page in the Poets & Writers directory for a rough notion of the publishing history. http://www.pw.org/content/rodney_nelson

DAVID L. O'NEAL: David L. O'Neal, a graduate of Princeton University, former Marine Corps officer, and retired rare book dealer, is now enjoying a second career as a writer, mostly of poetry. In addition to previous writing about rare books and book collecting, his recent creative work has been published in literary magazines such as

Bird Keeper, Sensations Magazine, Vision Magazine, The Eclectic Muse, Mississippi Crow, Quarterly, and *The Lyric,* and in such anthologies as *The Marin Poetry Center Anthology, Science Poetry, Nurturing Paws,* and *Voices of Bipolar Disorder.* O'Neal has also compiled *Babbling Birds: An Anthology of Poems About Parrots, From Antiquity to the Present,* which is the only book of its kind. His website is www. davidloneal.us

KRISTI PETERSEN SCHOONOVER: Kristi Petersen Schoonover's short fiction has appeared in *Carpe Articulum, The Adirondack Review, Barbaric Yawp, New Witch Magazine, Toasted Cheese,* and others, including several anthologies such as Dark Opus Press' *In Poe's Shadow.* She holds an MFA from Goddard College, has received three Norman Mailer Writers Colony Residencies, and is editor for *Read Short Fiction.* Her most recent work, *Skeletons in the Swimmin' Hole,* is a collection of ghost stories set in Disney Parks; her horror novel, *Bad Apple,* is forthcoming from Vagabondage Press. She's also a member of the New England Horror Writers Association. Her website is www.kristipetersenschoonover.com.

GLYN POPE: Glyn Pope grew up on a council estate in England. He studied theology at Nene University. Glyn interviewed Bob Marley the night before Marley cancelled his United Kingdom tour and went back to the warmth of Jamaica. Glyn has published articles for both Leonard Cohen and Bob Dylan "fan" magazines. A few years ago, he and his wife and daughter moved to France where he pursues a full time writing career. Last year, his successful novel *The Doctor, The Plutocrat, and The Mendacious Minister* was published by Cactus Rain in America. In September of 2012, he is organizing the first festival of literature in his home village of St Clementin, France. See http://glynpope.blogspot.com/

RICHARD T. RAUCH: Richard T. Rauch was born and raised in and around New Orleans, and after college and career stints in New York, Los Angeles, and Washington, D.C., returned to his native state, and currently lives along Bayou Lacombe in southeast Louisiana. Rick's poetry has appeared or is about to appear in *California Quarterly, decomP, Hotel Amerika, Many Mountains Moving, Meridian Anthology of Contemporary Poetry, The Old Red Kimono, The Oxford American, Quiddity, Slow Trains*, and *Westview*, among others.

ANJOLI ROY: Anjoli Roy writes creative nonfiction, fiction, and poetry, and is a recipient of the Myrle Clark Award for Creative Writing. Her work has appeared in *The Big Stupid Review, Brownstone Magazine, Diverse Voices Quarterly, ExPatLit.com: A Literary Review for Writers Abroad, Fiction365, Frontier Psychiatrist, Hawaiʻi Review, Hawaii Women's Journal, Midwest Literary Magazine*, and *The West Fourth Street Review*. Anjoli is a coeditor of *Vice-Versa: Creative Works and Comments* and the winter 2010 issue of *Mānoa: A Pacific Journal of International Writing*. Anjoli is a lecturer at St. Joseph's College in Brooklyn and is the grants coordinator at Girls Educational and Mentoring Services (GEMS). Visit her website at www.anjoliroy.com to read more of her work.

DON RUSS: Don Russ is the author of *Dream Driving* (Kennesaw State University Press, 2007) and the chapbook *Adam's Nap* (Billy Goat Press, 2005). He publishes widely and regularly in the literary magazines.

ELLEN SAVAGE: Ellen Savage's poetry has been recognized by Poets & Patrons and Highland Park Poetry. Her poems have appeared in *Calyx, East on Central, Avocet, Cram Poetry*, and *Butterfly Gardener*. Graduating in 1976 from the University of Illinois with a nursing degree, she has worked in obstetrical nursing through most of her career. It wasn't until 2007 when her son left for college that she began to devote serious time to writing. An avid bird watcher, she incorporates her love of the natural world in many of her poems. She lives in Highland Park, Illinois with her husband, Sean.

ROBERT SCOTELLARO: Robert Scotellaro's poetry and flash fiction have appeared in numerous journals and anthologies including *Battered Suitcase, Gargoyle, The Laurel Review, Red Rock*

Review, Willows Wept Review, and others. He is the author of five literary chapbooks. His most recent collections are *Rhapsody of Fallen Objects* (Flutter Press 2010) and *The Night Sings A Cappella* (Big Table Press 2011). He is the recipient of *Zone 3's* Rainmaker Award in Poetry. He is also the author of three books for children. He currently lives in San Francisco with his wife and daughter.

EMILY SEVERANCE: Emily Severance has an MFA in studio art from The School of the Art Institute of Chicago. Her poems have appeared or are forthcoming in *Camroc Press Review, Drunken Boat, Gargoyle, qarrtsiluni, Sisyphus,* and *Switched-on Gutenberg.* She teaches in New Mexico.

JENNIFER SMITH: Jennifer Smith is a resident of Los Angeles. She has her master's degree in English from Chapman Univeristy, and she teaches English at Los Angeles Valley College where she forces her students to read Rilke at least once during the semester.

COOPER SY: Cooper Sy studied poetry with Rachel Blau Du Plessis and then segued into film. She received her MFA in Film/TV from Temple University. A partial list of award winning films includes: *The Poet's Wife, Walking To Waldheim,* starring Doris Roberts and John Randolph, *Take Two* premiered at The American Film Institute. Recently, Cooper directed the play *Acts of Faith,* based on Grace Paley's short stories for Laterthanever Productions, San Diego. A documentary, *The Phoenix Effect,* received a grant from Leonard Nimoy and screened worldwide. Her short story "I'll Meet You At The Film Forum" was published Spring 2011 in *The Battered Suitcase.* This fall, Cooper is completing a novel and shooting the documentary *Five Privileged Chicks* in New York City. www.phoenixdocumentary.com

LORETTA SYLVESTRE: Loretta Sylvestre spent her early years in Southern California, but was later transplanted to the green, wet half of Washington State, where stories grow as wild as blackberries. She holds a bachelor's degree in Liberal Arts, from The Evergreen State

College. Her short fiction has appeared in a number of publications, in print and online. Her YA Fantasy novel *Beyond the Wizard's Threshold* was released in 2010. She also writes male/male romance under pen name Lou Sylvre.

CHERI L.R. TAYLOR: Cheri L.R. Taylor holds an MFA in Writing from Vermont College and is currently a writing instructor at Macomb College. She has four chapbooks of poetry and has been published in *Rattle, Ellipsis, Awakenings Review, The Café Review, Clean Sheets, Current Magazine, Third Wednesday*, and others. Her newest book, *Wolf Maiden Moon, a Tale in Thirteen Poems* was released from Pudding House Press in January of 2010. Director of The Blushing Sky Writer's Playground, Cheri works as an editor and a writing coach and hosts full-day writing workshops in the Metropolitan Detroit area. For more on Cheri, visit www.blushingskywrite.com.

JOHN TUSTIN: John Tustin is the divorced father of two perfect children. He graduated from nowhere, has no awards, and edits nothing. Fritzware.com/johntustinpoetry is a link to his poetry online.

V. ULEA: V. Ulea is a bilingual writer, a scholar, and a filmmaker. Her books have been published in the United States and Europe, including, most recently, a collection of short stories, *Snail* (Crossing Chaos: Canada, 2009). She is the editor of the anthology, *Quantum Works in the Planet of Arts* (Paraphilia: UK, 2010). Her works have appeared in *The Literary Review, The Bitter Oleander, Dream People, Sein und Werden*, and many others. Her books have received international awards. Her cycle of poems, *Letters from Another Planet*, has been nominated for the Pushcart Prize. She teaches courses on the art of decision-making in film, literature and the game of chess in the University of Pennsylvania.
http://www.v-ulea.net

MARK UNDERWOOD: Mark Underwood is a failed musician and part-time screenwriter. His first feature film *Forget Me Not* had its cinematic release in 2011 and is now available to download from all disreputable torrent sites. For the lesser-spotted band Yeti, Underwood wrote and sang songs including "Midnight Flight" and the unnecessarily abstract "Insect-Eating Man." For want of a better word, he "lives" in Muswell Hill, London with his neighbour's cat, Patch, where he spends his days shouting at apples and avoiding the mourning Joy.

GABRIEL VALJAN: Ronan Bennett short-listed Gabriel Valjan for the 2010 Fish Short Story Prize. Gabriel's short stories continue to appear in literary journals and online magazines. He recently won first prize in *ZOUCH* Magazine's inaugural Lit Bit Contest. His prose poems "Exile" will appear in *kill author,* edition 17 in February 2012. He lives in New England. *Roma, Underground*, his first novel, has been accepted by Winter Goose Publishers. The novel should be available in March 2012.

JULIE CATHERINE VIGNA: Julie Catherine Vigna is a freelance poet, writer and artist residing in Alberta, Canada. Writing and drawing have been driving passions throughout her life, which began in Dundas, Ontario, before she migrated to western Canada in 2004. She is inspired by the world around her, nature, and especially water—her muse and source of inspiration. Julie Catherine's poem, "Unremembered," was recently published in her local newspaper; another won a metaphorical poetry competition. She belongs to several internet writing groups, including 21st Century Poets, and has her own blog: *Muse-Sings, Poetry & Art of Julie Catherine*, at http://juliecatherinevigna.wordpress.com. She continues to write poetry, and is working on her first fiction novel for young adults; a mystery set in Georgian Bay, Ontario.

JOSEPH WADE: Joseph Wade is an eight-year military veteran, having spent three years in the Army and five years in the Navy. After the military, Joseph began his college education at Harrisburg Area Community College and is continuing his degree at Brooklyn College. Visit www.josephwade.com.

CAITLIN MEREDITH WALSH: Caitlin Meredith Walsh is a full-time college student in California. Her poetry has appeared in *StepAway Magazine* and in *Niteblade*. One of these poems was recently nominated for the Pushcart Prize, and another took second place in the Balticon 45 Poetry contest. When she's not writing, she devours good books, wanders through hard-to-access parts of town, and scavenges local secondhand shops looking for buried treasure.

MAGGIE WESTLAND: Maggie Westland loves all things verbally musical. Her work appears in print and online in America and England. Maggie has been featured at venues in southern California including Moorpark College where she is a member of the performance group, Razor Babes. Maggie's work has appeared in anthologies such as *Daybreak, Above us Only Sky*, and *If We Dance*, and has been critiqued via The Guardian Unlimited's Poetry Workshop. Her chapbook, *A Defiance of Daughters*, published by Conscious Ooze Press, is in Beyond Baroque's archive, Venice California. Maggie currently teaches poetry in Ventura County Schools with the SEASONS program. Google Maggie Westland to find more of her poetry, or visit her at www.maggiewestland.com

JOANNA M. WESTON: Joanna M. Weston has had poetry, reviews, and short stories published in anthologies and journals for twenty-five years. Her middle-reader, *Those Blue Shoes*, published by Clarity House Press; and poetry, *A Summer Father*, published by Frontenac House of Calgary. http://1960willowtree.wordpress.com/

ROBERT WEXELBLATT: Robert Wexelblatt is professor of humanities at Boston University's College of General Studies. He has published essays, stories, and poems in a wide variety of journals, two story collections, *Life in the Temperate Zone* and *The Decline of Our Neighborhood*, a book of essays, *Professors at Play*; his recent novel, *Zublinka Among Women*, won the Indie Book Awards First Prize for Fiction.

ANNE WHITEHOUSE: Anne Whitehouse is the author of the poetry collections *The Surveyor's Hand* (Compton Press), *Blessings and Curses* (Poetic Matrix Press), *Bear in Mind* (Finishing Line Press) and the just-published *One Sunday Morning* (Finishing Line Press). She is the author of the novel, *Fall Love*, now available as a free e-book from Feedbooks and Smashwords, as well as Amazon Kindle. You can find Anne online at www.annewhitehouse.com.

MARTIN WILLITTS JR.: Martin Willitts Jr. is a retired senior librarian. He was nominated for two Best of The Net awards and his fifth Pushcart Prize. He has had eight poetry chapbooks accepted in 2011, including *True Simplicity* (Poets Wear Prada Press, 2011), *My Heart Is Seven Wild Swans Lifting* (Slow Trains, 2011), *Why Women Are A Ribbon Around A Bomb* (Last Automat, 2011), *Art Is Always an Impression of What an Artist Sees* (Muse Café, 2011), *Protest, Petition, Write, Speak: Matilda Joslyn Gage Poems* (Matilda Joslyn Gage Foundation, 2011), *How To Find Peace* (Kattywumpus Press, 2011), *Swimming In The Ladle Of Stars* (Pudding House, 2011) and *Secrets No One Wants To Talk About* (Dos Madres Press, 2011).

BENJAMIN WOLFE: Benjamin Wolfe spent a nomadic childhood hopping from place to place across the tropical continent of Asia, all in pursuit of his expatriate father. The sights and sounds of the countries in which he found himself, and the constant process of uprooting and relocation, gave him a fascination for the unknown and a low tolerance for boredom. And a conviction that life must be an adventure. Returning from Asia, he studied history at university in London. Since graduating, he has written freelance theatre reviews for a local paper and penned romantic poetry in his spare time, all the while plotting his escape back to the tropics in search of fame and fortune.

45324770R00090

Made in the USA
San Bernardino, CA
05 February 2017